T0353931

WE, US, OUR

RON MARCOTTE

authorHOUSE®

AuthorHouse™
1663 Liberty Drive
Bloomington, IN 47403
www.authorhouse.com
Phone: 833-262-8899

Published by AuthorHouse   11/05/2024

ISBN: 979-8-8230-3261-2 (sc)
ISBN: 979-8-8230-3260-5 (e)

Library of Congress Control Number: 2024917740

Print information available on the last page.

CONTENTS

PREAMBLE---A LITTLE WALK HERE AND THERE BEFORE WE START

Every weekend when I go to church I read these words, "Surrender the I, me, mine and strive for the we, us, our." This entire book is an attempt to explain those words, to get to the real meaning, which is extremely beneficial for all of us.

Here's the first example. This is not my book, but ours, yours, and mine. I'm presenting important topics, but you can add to them. Just make sure it's the truth because that's what's important and will set us free.

Also, don't dismiss this as simple religion. True religion doesn't end on Saturday or Sunday. It goes throughout the week. Saturday or Sunday is when Christians, Jews, Muslims, most denominations meet to give a united expression of adoration to the one God, the Creator of all of us and the universe. Each of the other days of the week are also important in expressing individually this adoration and in serving God and all other human beings. Do you understand the weekend and the week in this manner? Do you meet weekly for that expression? Has our culture understood this perspective?

A recent sermon preached by a deacon says much of what I want to say. Christ has called himself "The Good Shepherd." We are the sheep. He came to earth to save all of us, like the sheep, to re-unite us with our true Father, the Creator of each of us. When I looked at the congregation, I couldn't tell who was going to be rescued because the response needed was love, inside each person. To be reunited with our Creator there are two essential commands of Christ for all humans: "Love the Lord your God with all your heart and with all your soul and with all your strength and with all your mind" and 'Love your neighbor as yourself." Luke 10:27 That means all other human beings. We all heard the same words, but the response is inside each of us.

Women are recognized as being more emotional than men, so the first part, the heart part, may be theirs more than men. One reason is motherhood. Take away the "M" from "Mother" and what do you have: "Other". Consider the nine months of pregnancy. The mother and child are one physically. That must affect the mother's emotions.

The purpose of this book is to help us see God in his universe more clearly.

---It will cost you. It has cost me, rising at 2:22 or 3:33 to listen in the night's silence to hear what I should write and then the effort to get it written and published. You will have to read this in the same manner, in silence, at a cost to you, but it should be worth it.

---We see God in the Beatitudes, truly studying each one to see how we are to love in all matters.

---We see God in the Scriptures. For a large part, it is Christ's words.

---We see God in nature every day of our lives. I heard the thunder the other day and realized once more that no other being, especially not a human, could make that sound.

---We see God in all human beings. Each is unique, different, special.

---We can see God through the Latin language as well. "Deus" in Latin means God in English. "Dei" means "of God" in English. Some people have come up with a program of "d e i" as diversity, equality. and inclusion. "Of God" can be seen in that diversity is of God, our Father and Creator of his diverse human creations, equality is of Jesus Christ His Son, Who will judge us all on the basis of equality as in Matthew 25, and the Holy Spirit, Love, can be seen in inclusion, not closing our eyes on anyone as in Matthew 25 and seeing all humans as His creations, whether we understand them or not.

Matthew 5:1-12, the Beatitudes, and Matthew 25:31-46, the consequences of seeing all of God's creations or not seeing them, are crucial readings for all human beings.

Christ's words in hymn form are very clear "Whatsoever you do to the least of My brethren, that you do unto me."

Let's begin with looking at the Beatitudes taken together and then separately. Then we can take a history quiz about the Presidents in my lifetime. And finally we can look at our tribalism, the new fad.

PART ONE: THE   BEATITUDES

This is my understanding of the Beatitudes. Together, they constitute love, so I will present them in their entirety here, go through each individually afterwards, and then present the flow again at the end of this first part. I will also present what we have seen from 2016 to 2021, the antithesis to the Beatitudes, the exact opposite.

THE FLOW

HUMILITY

This is the foundation, the basis

I recognize I'm one of 8,000,000,000 human creations

at present time of one CREATOR.

EMPATHY

So, I can relate to others, my equals, understand
them, feel what they feel

MEEKNESS

So, I want to serve them, even unto death, to provide

for their needs because their needs are like my needs.

JUSTICE

So, I want them to have at least equal to what I have,

not more, not less.

MERCY

So, if my Creator can forgive me for my offenses, the

least I can do is forgive any other person for misdeeds against me.

PURITY

So, I need clarity of spiritual vision, seeing everyone, not

missing anyone, and seeing everyone's full worth.

PEACEMAKER

So, this is the final goal for all of us,

a prerequisite of love.

COURAGE

So, I must act boldly, proclaiming Christ

as THE WAY, THE TRUTH, THE LIFE

leading to AGAPE, E I ERNAL LOVE.

Beatitude One	HUMILITY
Christ's Words	"Blessed are the poor in spirit for theirs is the kingdom of heaven." Matthew 5:3
Christ's Actions	Bethlehem Nazareth Golgotha

The Antithesis	ARROGANCE
Trump's Words	"Nobody in the history of this country has ever known so much about Infrastructure as Donald Trump." July, 2016

There's nobody bigger or better at the military than I am." June, 2015

"I know more about ISIS (the Islamic State militant group} than the generals do" Nov, 2015

He claimed to know more than the majority of scientists about the climate.

He claimed to know more about the economy than the professionals.

He said these words about himself, from Aaron Blake's article, "19 Things Donald Trump Knows Better Than Anyone Else."   1

Trump's Actions   Trump is the "I" of the storm that we need to see. Pun
                         intended.

                         Trump Tower   Washington, D.C.   Mar-A-Lago

Do you see humility, truth in everything Christ said and did and do you not see
arrogance in Trump's words and actions?

Beatitude Two	EMPATHY
Christ's Words	Blessed are those who mourn for they will be comforted." Matthew 5:4
Christ's Actions	Changed water into wine at Cana, healed the sick and the lepers, gave sight to the blind and hearing to the deaf, and raised the dead back to life.
The Antithesis	APATHY
Trump's Words	"I'm the best thing that ever happened to Puerto Rico. Nobody even close." In 2020. 2
Trump's Actions	Tossed rolls of paper at Puerto Ricans who had suffered through the hurricanes He held back 13 billion dollars in aid to Puerto Rico from 2017 after the hurricanes Irma and Maria until 2020 as the elections approached.

Beatitude Three   MEEKNESS

Christ's Words   "Blessed are the meek for they will inherit the earth."
                         Matthew 5:5

Christ's Actions   Golgotha, a crown of thorns, a heavy crucifix, three
                         hours of hands and feet nailed to the cross

The Antithesis   SELFISHNESS

Trump's Words   "What's in it for me?" 3

Trump's Actions   Everything he does is for his profit, even when he's
                         being held to account.

Beatitude Four	JUSTICE
Christ's Words	"Blessed are those who hunger and thirst for righteousness, for they will be filled." Matthew 5:6
Christ's Actions	Talked with everyone. Helped everyone who sought help.
The Antithesis	INJUSTICE
Trump's Words	"There are good people on both sides." After the murder at Charlottesville, Virginia. 4
Trump's Actions	Favored the whites, the Scandinavians. Cursed the blacks and Latinos.

Beatitude Five	ETERNAL MERCY
Christ's Words	"Blessed are the merciful, for they will be shown mercy." Matthew 5:7
Christ's Actions	In granting His mercy, Christ promised the criminal that he would be in Christ's eternal kingdom that very day.
The Antithesis	TEMPORAL MERCY
Trump's Words	"I've never done anything wrong." 5
Trump's Actions	He pardoned Manafort, Flynn, Stone, Bannon not because they were sorry for their crimes but because they remained loyal to him. 6

Beatitude Six	PURITY OF VISION
Christ's Words	"Blessed are the pure in spirit, for they will see God." Matthew 5:8
Christ's Actions	He talked with the Samaritan woman at the well, knew her life's history, and the conversation ended by urging her conversion with "sin no more."
The Antithesis	IMPURITY
Trump's Words	"When you're a star...you can do anything to women." And the famous conversation with Access Hollywood. 7
Trump's Actions	Affairs with Stormy Daniels, E. Jean Carroll, three marriages.

Beatitude Seven	PEACEMAKING
Christ's Words	"Blessed are the peacemakers, for they will be called sons of God." Matthew 5:9
Christ's Actions	Brought the Holy Spirit to the Apostles when they were gathered together in fear after his death and he removed that fear so they could bring peace to others.
The Antithesis	CHAOS
Trump's Words	Called Putin "a genius." after invading Ukraine. 8
Trump's Actions	Didn't criticize Putin's invasion of Ukraine, which isn't simply not loving your neighbor, but brought harm to over 3,000,000 neighbors. 3,000,000 human beings!!

Beatitude Eight	COURAGE
Christ's Words	"Blessed are those who are persecuted because of righteousness, for theirs is the kingdom of heaven. "Matthew 5:10
Christ's Actions	Attacked because he spoke the truth. He had come to provide us with love, not temporal riches.
The Antithesis	FEAR
Trump's Words	They're 'Suckers" and "Losers" who save others. 9
Trump's Actions	Fear of losing political support is his cudgel.

Let's 'Surrender the I, me, mine, and strive for the we, us, our."

THE FLOW

HUMILITY

This is the foundation, the basis.

We recognize that we're part of 8,000,000,000 human beings.

EMPATHY

So, we can relate to others, our equals, understand them,

feel what they feel

MEEKNESS

So, we want to serve them, even unto death, to provide for

their needs because their needs are like our needs

JUSTICE

So, we want them to have at least equal to what we have,

not more, not less

MERCY

So, if our Creator can forgive us for our sins, the least

we can do is forgive any other person

for misdeeds against us

PURITY

So, we need clarity of spiritual vision to see everyone,

not missing anyone

and seeing everyone's full worth

PEACEMAKING

So, this is the final goal of all of us,

a prerequisite for love

COURAGE

So, we must act boldly, proclaiming Christ as

THE WAY, THE TRUTH, THE LIFE,

Leading to AGAPE, ETERNAL LOVE

PART TWO: PRESIDENTS

Franklin D. Roosevelt, 1933-1945   CAPABILITY

FDR's Words	"The only thing we have to fear is fear itself." 10
	"The Presidency is ... preeminently a place of moral leadership." 11
FDR's Actions	He faced and overcame the Great Depression----his first pandemic.
	---1935 Created the WPA, the Works Progress Administration putting millions to work.
	---1935 Signed the Social Security Act, which continues to help Americans to this day.
FDR's Words	"December 7, 1941, a day that will live in infamy."
	"In the future days, which we seek to make secure, we look forward to a world founded upon four essential freedoms." 12
FDR's Actions	---December 8, 1941, the United States declared war against Japan, which had launched the raid on Pearl Harbor the day before, killing 2400 persons, wounding 1200, and destroying many battleships and airplanes. Roosevelt had his second pandemic, along with the dictatorships of Hitler's Germany and Mussolini's Italy. It would take the entire nation's concerted effort until 1945 to overcome this pandemic.
	---Gave America and the world four freedoms: 1) of speech, the freedom to speak up, 2) of religion, to practice our particular religion, 3} from want, the freedom from hunger, and 4) from fear, from the bullying of dictators 13

Trump's Words   January 22, 2018 "We have it totally under control. It's one person coming in from China. It's going to be just fine."   14

"I couldn't tell them what I knew" in a taped interview with Bob Woodward.   15

Trump's Actions   ---Covid-19 was the pandemic that Trump faced in his Presidency. Some of his actions were helpful, but overall the full effort required to defeat it was not presented to us.

When Joe Biden became President in 2021, the number of deaths from the pandemic was still on the rise and would continue to over one million, greater than the number of deaths in the Civil War of 1865.   16

---He tried to give us four enslavements: - 1) from speech - an enslavement to lies by bombarding us with them,

2) an enslavement to religion by imposing his cult on us and not letting us make our own moral decisions with our God,

3) an enslavement to want if we embraced his concern for money, money, money,

4) an enslavement to fear him and his political power.

These are just exactly the opposite of

the four freedoms FDR presented.

Harry S. Truman, 1945-1953   **HONESTY**

Truman's Words	"The buck stops here." 17
Truman's Action's	To end World War II, Truman had to make a decision: use atomic bombs against Hiroshima and Nagasaki or continue the war at considerable cost of lives to both the Japanese and Americans. History will forever hold him responsible for choosing to unveil horrific power into the modern era. However, there is a major difference between Truman's acts and Netanyahu's war now. Truman was not out to exterminate the Japanese and Hirohito accepted the signs of American power. He surrendered.
	Hamas, the ruler of the Gazans, will not surrender. Their goal is to exterminate the Israelis, as stated in their governing documents. Both Hamas and Israel need to accept the two State solution to end the war.
Truman's Words	"I never gave anybody Hell. I just told the truth on those fellows and they thought it was Hell." 18
Truman's Actions	---He promoted the Marshall Plan to help our allies after World War II.
	---He aided the South Koreans in stopping the North Koreans aggression into taking over South Korea.
	---He fired General Douglas MacArthur for trying to lead us to war with China. 19

Trump's Words   "I don't take responsibility at all" in regard to Covid-19.
                     20

Trump's Actions   Did some good things, such as appointing Pence's staff
                     and authorizing vaccines, but failed to quarantine and
                     promote face masks to stop the spread.

Trump's Words   "I couldn't tell them what I knew" in a taped interview
                     about Covid-19. 21

Trump's Actions   The Washington Post checked for a fact that Trump told
                     over30,000 lies during his Presidency.   22

Dwight D. Eisenhower, 1953-1961   PEACEMAKER

Eisenhower's Words   "The United States never lost a soldier or a foot of
                          ground in my administration. We kept the peace.
                          People asked how it happened—by God, it didn't just
                          happen, I'll tell you that."   23

Eisenhower's Actions   ---In 1956, Israel captured "the whole of the Gaza Strip
                          and the Sinai Peninsula. The British began air raids on
                          Egypt over the Suez Canal " and Eisenhower condemned
                          It. The United Nations voted "to mobilize police force to
                          restore peace in Egypt."

                          ---The Korean War ended "with an armistice creating a
                          demilitarized zone and a mutual exchange of prisoners
                          of war. Casualties for the war were approximately
                          150,000 Americans, 900,000 Chinese, and 2,000,000
                          Koreans."

                          ---SEATO, the South-East Asia Treaty Organization, was
                          formed. 24

Eisenhower's Words   "I can think of nothing more boring for the American
                          public than to have to sit in their living rooms for a
                          whole half an hour looking at my face on their" TV's. 25

Eisenhower Actions   ---In 1955, signed "the bill amending Fair Labor
                          Standards Act to raise the minimum wage to $1 per
                          hour."

                          ---In 1953, "in his speech at the United Nations,
                          Eisenhower proposes his 'Atoms for

                          Peace' Program'."

---In 1956, "eighty -two nations at the United Nations agree on a new international Atomic Energy Agency."

---In 1957, the Supreme Court ordered "the desegregation of schools" and "a federal court" had to tell Arkansas to withdraw its national guard which had prevented nine black students from entering.

Violence followed when the National Guard left, but

Eisenhower sent federal troops to restore order.   26

Donald J. Trump, 2016-2020   CHAOS

Trump's Words   "I know more than the Generals."   27

The captured and dead are "Losers," "Suckers." 28

Trump's Actions   There was no peace in Charlottesville. Virginia the night a woman was run over by a car belonging to a member of a white racist organization.

John F. Kennedy, 1961-1963	UNSELFISHNESS
Kennedy's Words	"And so. my fellow Americans. Ask not what your country can do for you--ask what you can do for your country." 29
	'We stand for freedom. That is our conviction for ourselves; that is our only commitment to others." 30
Kennedy's Actions	---Urged Congress "to shoot for the moon," to overtake the Russian plan, giving hope to Americans that we will reach the moon first, a positive attitude that was felt throughout the United States.
	---In 1961, created the Peace Corps, providing opportunities for young people to volunteer for projects to help throughout the world, a positive attitude.
	--In 1961, the United States and Latin American countries formed the Alliance for Progress to promote social and political reform throughout Latin America, another positive, hopeful program.
	Made mistakes in the Bay of Pigs invasion of Cuba. 31

Trump's Words

"I 'm going to give a big beautiful present for Christmas."   32

"I want my people to listen to me like Kim Jung Un's people listen to him."   33

Trump's Actions

The Christmas present was for the rich, the wealthy, and for himself: a tax bill that lowered the amount the wealthy paid in regular taxes from 35% to 21 % for corporations and cut estate taxes in half, leaving the country in debt with an estimated $1.46 trillion over a ten year period.   34

Lyndon B. Johnson, 1963-1969   JUSTICE

Johnson's Words   "The "Great Society rests on abundance and liberty for
                           all. It demands an end of poverty and racial justice."
                           35

Johnson's Actions   This statesman from Texas, a Southerner, will always be
                           remembered in history fortwo things, one a failure, his
                           escalating the war in Vietnam,   and two, an actual push
                           for an ideal in The Great Society, "a nation free of
                           poverty and racial division."   36

Donald J. Trump's, 2016-2020   INJUSTICE

Trump' Words   What he called Haiti everyone knows and what he said
                           about Latinos is: "They're bringing drugs. They're
                           bringing crime. They're rapists. And some, I assume,
                           are good people."   37

Trump's Actions   By supporting a white supremacy agenda, David Duke
                           and others state clearly that they are simply following
                           the directives of an American President.   38

Richard M. Nixon, 1959-1964　　　IMPEACHMENT HEARING

Nixon's Words　　　　"Always remember others may hate you but those who hate you don't win unless you hate them."　39

Nixon's Actions　　　---Unfortunately, Nixon didn't listen to the words of advice that he said above and instead focused on the Democrats as his enemies, hating them, breaking into the Watergate, which brought about his impeachment.

---Brought about normalization of relations with China.

---Ended the Vietnam War. 40

Donald J. Trump, 2016-2020　　　IMPEACHMENT HEARINGS

Trumps's Words　　　"Crooked Hillary," "Crazy Bernie," "Lying" Ted Cruz, "Nutjob" Lindsey.　41

Trump's Actions　　　Demeaned his political opponents, Republicans as well as Democrats, and succeeded in getting his followers to hate his political opponents.　42

Gerald R. Ford, 1974-1977   SIMPLICITY

Ford's Words   "Truth is the glue that holds government together.
                           Compromise is the oil that makes government go."
                           43

Ford's Actions   He pardoned Nixon.   44

Donald J. Trump, 2016-2020   DUPLICITY

Trump's Words   "The insurrection on January 6 was by peaceful people."
                                    45

Trump's Actions   He wants to pardon himself without recognizing his
                           crimes. He said he would even pardon those convicted
                           of crimes on January 6.   46

James E. Carter, 1977-1981   INTEGRITY

Carter's Words

"In his day, Jesus broke down walls of separation and superiority among people. 47"

The passage of the civil rights act during the 1960's was the greatest thing to happen to the South in my lifetime. It lifted a burden from the whites as well as the blacks." 48

"War may sometimes be a necessary evil. But no matter how necessary, it is always an evil, never a good. We will not learn how to live together in peace by killing each other's children." 49

Carter's Actions

---The Camp David Accords, which brought Israel and Egypt to a peace agreement.

---An attempt to storm Iran by a small contingent of American forces failed and Carter was held responsible. 50

Donald J. Trump, 2016-2020   ABSENCE OF INTEGRITY

Trump's Words   "I'm not sure I have ever asked God's forgiveness…
                              When I go to church and when I drink my little wine and
                              have my little cracker, I guess that is a form of
                              forgiveness. I do that as often as I can because I feel
                              cleansed."   52

Trump's Actions   Demeaning, creating enmity and fear, separating
                              immigrant parents and children. 5153

Reagan's Words

"Government can and must provide opportunity, not smother it, foster productivity, not stifle it. " 53

"We welcome change and openness for we believe that freedom and security go together, that the advance of human liberty can only strengthen the cause of world peace. There is one sign the Soviets can make that would be unmistakable, that would advance dramatically the cause of freedom and peace. General Secretary Gorbachev, if you seek peace, if you seek prosperity for the Soviet Union and Eastern Europe, if you seek liberalization, come here to this Gate! Mr. Gorbachev, tear down this Wall." 54

Reagan's Actions

----Reagan fired 13,000 air traffic controllers when they went on strike..

---Considered the Speaker of the House, a Democrat, as one of his best friends

---Shot by a would-be assassin.

---Instituted Reaganomics in the economy, involving tax cuts and cutting federal funding.

---Sent forces to liberate the island of Grenada from atheistic Communism.

---Figured in the Iran-Contra scandal, involving the secret sale of arms to Iran and the use of those funds to help the Contras fight Communism in Nicaragua 55

Trump's Words

"I would build a great wall and no one builds walls better than me, believe me, and I'll build them very inexpensively. I will build a great wall and I'll have Mexico pay for it." 56

Trump's Actions

Trump got money to build his wall from Congress, the military budget, and individual donors, but not from Mexico. The original estimates ranged from a one time payment of 8 billion dollars to 28 billion dollars.

His friend, Steve Bannon, was convicted for siphoning off money from individual donors.

The entire southern border of the United States is over 1900 miles. With Trump's wall, we now have a wall of less than 600 miles.   Would a more effective use of the money be to provide more border personnel and more judges?   57

George H. W. Bush, 1989-1993   INTERNATIONAL PROGRESS

Bush's Words	"America is never wholly herself unless she is engaged in high moral principle. We as a people have such a purpose today. It is to make kinder the face of the nation and gentler the face of the world." 58
Bush's Actions	Three major achievements

  --helped in ending the Cold War with Russia

  ---ousted Panama's dictator, Manuel Noriega

  ---led an international effort to victory in the Persian War   59

Trump's Words	"America first." 60
Trump's Actions	---Imposed tariffs on China, which China retaliated by

  Imposing tariffs on their goods shipped to us

  ---Tried to dissolve NAFTA

  ==separated from our allies in demanding they pay their costs in NATO   61

William J. Clinton, 1993-2001   COHESION

Clinton's Words   "I ask you to join in a re-United States. We need to
                             empower our people so they can take more
                             responsibility for their own lives in a world that is ever
                             smaller, where everyone counts... We need a new spirit
                             of community, a sense that we are all in this together, or
                             the American Dream will continue to wither. Our
                             destiny is bound up with the destiny of every other
                             American." 62

Clinton's Actions   ---signed the Family and Medical Leave Act

                            ---helped in the peace accord between Israel's Yitzak
                            Rabin and Palestine's Yasser Arafat

                            ---signed the Brady Handgun Act

                            ----signed the north American Free Trade Agreement
                            (NAFTA)

                            ---began Operation Desert Fox against Saddam Hussein

                            ---authorized Operation Allied Force against the Serbian
                            assault on Albanian Muslims

                            ----impeached for the Monica Lewinsky affair   63

Donald J. Trump, 2016-2020   DIVISION

Trump's Words   ---one word "Vermin"   It says a lot.   Where did he
                                 get that word? Was it from Hitler's book <u>Mein Kamph</u>?
                                 Does he keep that book alongside his bed?   64

Trump's Actions   ---He has said he wants to be a dictator "for one day".
                                 Or is it more, like Hitler? 65

George W. Bush, 2001-2009   UPHELD AMERICAN IDEALS

                                FOUGHT FOREIGN TERRORISM

Bush's Words   "America has never been united by blood or birth or
                                soil. We are bound by ideals that move us beyond our
                                backgrounds, lift us above our interests and teach us
                                what it means to be citizens. Every child must be taught
                                these principles. Every citizen must uphold them. And
                                every immigrant, by embracing these ideals, makes our
                                country more, not less American."   66

                                "Terrorist attacks can shake the foundations of our
                                buildings, but they cannot touch the foundations of
                                America. These acts shatter steel, but they cannot dent
                                the steel of American resolve." 67

Bush's Actions   ---fought against foreign terrorism led by Osama Bin
                                Laden and the Taliban.   68

Donald. J. Trump, 2016-2029   DENIGRATED AMERICAN IDEALS

                                INSTIGATED DOMESTIC TERRORISM

Trump's Words   "It was a lovefest between the Capitol Police and the
                                people that walked down to the Capitol."   69

Trump's Actions   Was "practically and morally responsible" for bringing
                                domestic terrorism to this country for his personal self-
                                interest.   70

Barack H. Obama, 2009-2017   CONCERN FOR ALL AMERICANS

Obama's Words   " We are reminded that, in the fleeting time we have on
                             this earth, what matters is not wealth, or status, or
                             power or fame. But rather how well we have loved and
                             what small part we have played in making the lives of
                             other people better>" 71

Obama's Actions   ---passed the Affordable Care Act providing health care
                             for millions

                             ---removed Muammar Gaddafi from Libya and
                             terminated Osama Bin Laden

                             ---signed a treaty with Iran to prevent it from becoming
                             a nuclear threat

                             ---appointed two women to the Supreme Court, Sonia
                             Sotomayor and Elena Kagan   72

Donald J. Trump, 2016-2020   CONCERN FOR HIMSELF ONLY

Trump's Words   "I could stand in the middle of Fifth Avenue and shoot
                             somebody, and I wouldn't lose any voters, OK? It's like
                             incredible."   73

Trump's Actions   ---tried to repeal Obama's Affordable Care Act, although
                             he had nothing to replace it

                             ---demeaned John McCain for opposing him   74

                             ---promoted racial division throughout the country   75

                             ---opposed Latino immigration through separation of
                             children from parents 76

                             ---unilaterally withdrew from the Iran treaty 77

                             ---promoted loss of faith in our democratic system for
                             his attempted autocratic takeover 78

PART THREE: TRIBALISM

The word "tribalism" has come into our current vocabulary. It wasn't a word I used much during my lifetime but it has become increasingly popular. What it does connote is division, separation into particular groups that are more important to us than being Christians or Americans so I do not like the importance "tribalism" has undertaken.

This final section deals with it mainly because Trump's words and actions have promoted the word, "Trumpism." This is the most difficult part of my writing and to get through it, those who know me well will know that I have to sing softly two little ditties. The first is from Bing Crosby: "Ya gotta accentuate the positive, eliminate the negative, and don't mess with Mr. In-between." The second is my own: "I don't wanna, but I gotta, so I'm gonna."

The "accentuate the positive" is in the Beatitudes which form love. I want to be a true Christian and a moral American. The Beatitudes are the way to our eternal reward. An adherence to the Constitution is the way for our temporal reward. The Preamble states: " "We hold these truths to be self-evident, that all men are created equal, that they are endowed by their Creator with certain inherent, inalienable rights, that among these are life, liberty, and the pursuit of happiness." Re-read this sentence and note the words "equal," "created", "Creator", and "rights." for an unforgettable understanding.

The "eliminate the negative" means getting rid of their antithesis, their opposite. How can we do that? It would seem that the only way now to get rid of Trumpism is for a strong majority of us to vote against Trump in 2024. The wheels of justice from the legal system are moving very slowly. As Christians, we believe that we must hate the sin, but love the sinner. We are not failing in love when we don't vote for him. We are keeping him from perpetrating more evil.

To help towards "eliminating the negative" requires courage, the eighth Beatitude on the part of the author and the publisher. We need to appeal with urgency that certain "trlbes" act firmly in rejecting Trumpism.

CHRISTIANS AS A "TRIBE"

I believe that no Christian should vote for Trump to be our President. Why? Please think and be honest. The truth can set us free. In studying the Beatitudes, we can see that he is the antithesis, the opposite of Christ's attitudes for love of God.

Yesterday, May 15, 2024, I was driving in the Villages and saw an ad on a flashing billboard that disturbed me. The word "GOD" caught my attention immediately. The full message was "GOD and Donald Trump save this nation."

Trump is a human being and, like you and me, of himself he is not divine , and I do not believe that he has divine power as our God, to whom we sing, as Christians, "How Great Thou Art" in absolute awe , so I did not like the implication that he has divine power to save us also.

As Christians, we believe that Jesus Christ was both human and divine, part of the Trinity, one of three, Father, Son, and Holy Spirit. We pray the Apostles' Creed: "I believe in God the Father, Creator of heaven and earth…and in Jesus Christ, his Only Son…I believe in the Holy Spirit…." Read the entire Creed. Re-read the Scriptures to understand that Christ demonstrated clearly that he was divine. He loved his Father and all humans even to the death on Golgotha.

The Jewish leaders rejected Christ as divine precisely because he didn't give them the wealth and the power they wanted and believed the Messiah would give them. His kingdom was not of this world.

Trump's attraction is precisely the opposite "money, money, money" and "power, power, power," here on earth, all temporal and limited.   Christ's kingdom is eternal and timeless.

Truth and morality are important and I believe that many non-Christians, Jews,

39

Muslims, Buddhists, agnostics, often may be searching for both truth and morality sometimes more than "Christians" in name only. A true Christian observes the two commands of Christ, love of God above all else and love of neighbor.

We all saw the many accomplishments of Donald Trump and some of us believe they were neither Christian nor American.

He revolutionized politics   The Republican Party was transformed

                              into the Trump Party.

He established a human   McConnell, Barr, Pompeo, Graham and

cult, not divine worship   others turned into sycophants. Hannity,

                              Carlson, Ingraham, Coulter, others, into

                              misinformation providers.

He overwhelmed us   He blinded us with glitz and showmanship. He took us for a ride through many stop signs.

He sold us   Fear

                              Greed

                              Selfishness

                              Lies

                              Hatred

                              Immorality

                              Racism

                              Violence

                              Autocracy,

By convincing us not to believe	An insurrection on January 6, 2021
what we were seeing	The devastation of COVID-19.
	The power and evil of Putin, Kim Jung Un, Erdogan
	The dismantling of our governing
	institutions, Congress, DOJ, State
	The misuse of taxes, tariffs, emoluments.

And he will do even more with the plan that his associates have completed for him, Project 2025, a detailed plan, step by step, to accomplish his goals.

EMPATHY---IMMIGRANTS AND NATIVES AS A "TRIBE"

I believe that no immigrant or native should vote for Trump to be our President, our chief representative. Why? Because of who we are.

We are a nation of immigrants. Were you, your parents, or your ancestors immigrants? Millions of Germans, Italians, French, Irish passed through Ellis Island in New York between 1900 to 1914. It's estimated that 5,000 to 10,000 immigrants passed daily through its gates from 1892 to 1954. In 1886, President Grover Cleveland dedicated the Statue of Liberty as a gift from the French to honor our country for what it provided. 79 Emma Lazarus wrote the sonnet that is at the base of this statue, a true symbol of America's greatness, "Give me your tired, your poor, Your huddled masses yearning to breathe free, the wretched refuse of your teeming shore. Send these, the homeless, tempest-tossed to me. I lift my lamp beside the golden door." 80

Go back to the "Mayflower," a ship that brought a small but important group to the United States seeking freedom. These helped to start our history as a nation, but they also received help from the natives with whom they often clashed. The treatment of native Americans is not a part of why we should be proud of our American heritage. Nor is the treatment of passengers on other ships who were to be used as slaves for menial work. This was not the freedom our country offered to the "huddled masses," but it is the truth, and we must make up for it by ensuring freedom now to these "tribes."

Donald Trump is correct that we have a problem at the southern border, but he uses it for his personal political gain. First, I believe that he exaggerates the problem . If he believes that the problem is so great he would have welcomed immediately Senator James Lankford's proposal in February. Senator Lankford is a Republican Senator from Oklahoma and his bill was bi-partisan. It provided funding to build the wall, increase technology at the border, and add more detention beds, more agents , and more deportation flights. But Trump did not want anything that seemed good for Americans during the Biden administration, so he instructed his Senators to vote against the bill and he would use it as a political talking point up to November, a 10 month delay. 81

MEEKNESS---THE MILITARY AS A "TRIBE"

I believe that no member of the military should vote for Trump to be
our President. Why? First of all because of the true and full meaning
of these words: "America is the land of the free because of the
brave." We citizens experience freedom because of the sacrifice of
those in the military. The initial sacrifice generally is family life, but
the ultimate sacrifice may be life itself, as our history has shown.

The members of the military do not need a commander -in-chief who
asks "What's in it for them?" They should not want for that
command to supposedly have avoided their service because of "bone
spurs." They might want to listen to what certain Generals and
Admirals, their true commanders and models, have said
about Trump.

General Colin Powell   "We have a Constitution, and we have to follow the
                          Constitution, and the President has drifted away

                          from it. He lies about things . And he gets away with it
                          because people will not hold him accountable." 70

General Jim Mattis   "...the U.S. is suffering the consequences of three years
                          without mature leadership. Trump was the first
                          President in his lifetime who does not even pretend to
                          unify the nation. Instead, he tries to divide us." 71

General John Kelley Chief of Staff Trump Presidency	"I think we need to look harder at who we elect. I think we should look at people that are running for office and put them through the filter. What is their character like? What is their ethics? 72
Admiral Mike Mullen Joint Chiefs Chairman Bush Presidency	He was "Sickened" by what he saw at Lafayette Square when Trump forced the military to interrupt a protest of George Floyd's death. It was "impossible to remain silent." Trump "laid bare his disdain for the rights of peaceful protest in this country, gave succor to the leaders of other countries who take comfort in our domestic strife and risked further politicizing the men and women of our armed services.' 73
Marine General Josh Allen	Stated his fear that Trump's actions might signal the "beginning of the end of the of the American Experiment." 74
Admiral William McRaven Special Operations Commander	"We are not the most powerful nation in the world because of our aircraft carriers, carriers, our economy or our seat at the United Nations Security Council. We are

the most powerful nation because our ideals of universal freedom and equality have been backed up by our belief that we were champions of justice, the protectors of the less fortunate." 75

JUSTICE---BLACKS AS A "TRIBE"

I believe that no black should vote for Trump to be our President, our chief representative. Why? Because we are not simply a nation of whites, English, Germans, Irish, Scots, Norse, but we are a nation of mixed colors, black, brown, red, yellow hued citizens as well as whites, all of whom deserve love and respect.

Nathaniel Philbrick has done a masterful work in providing us with the history of the white hued Americans who came to this country on The Mayflower ship in 1620. 88 One year before, however, in 1619, another ship arrived with a small contingent of blacks who were to be used as slaves. We owe a debt of gratitude to Nikole-Hannah Jones for Project 1619 launched through the New York Times. 89 As a student of history, I believe both studies are important. The truth is important and the facts are that we have a history of contributions from Americans of various skin colors.

We had a Civil War back in the 1860's over that slavery issue. It wasn't good for either side, but it's the truth, factual, so we have to learn from it. Maybe our children will learn from it. Progress has come slowly, bringing us to our times.

John Lewis was a fellow Protestant Christian seminarian while I was a Roman Catholic Christian seminarian, and to this day I stand in awe of him. Our love of Christ may have been the same, but he way outperformed me in seeking justice with extreme courage. I totally respect him for it. He was famous for "good trouble.," particularly in seeking civil rights for all humans.

Once he was arrested for protesting at a restaurant by simply refusing to leave until he was served. He was taken to jail, and after some time, he was driven to the state line. 90 If I had gone to pick him up, this would have been our conversation. John: "Drive me right back to that restaurant. Ron: "What the heck, John? Are you crazy? They'll just arrest you again." John: "I know, but I can't stop until we receive equal justice." I reluctantly but hopefully would have driven him back for another peaceful protest. Would you have driven him back?

This is just one occasion. There are so many others over many years, centuries of injustice. Good events, like the Martin Luther King, Jr. rally in Washington, D.C with the approval of John F. Kennedy during his Presidency. But there continue to be the opposite signs, such as the George Floyd incident. It was an unfortunate death as seen by some; murder as seen by others. Paying a store owner a false $20 bill should not result in a person's termination of life.

Donald Trump once asked a young black male, "What do you have to lose?" by voting for him. The right answer would have been, "My integrity, my personhood as a black American, my fellowship with my brothers, such as John Lewis, my hope for justice as soon as possible."

Would this have been the correct answer? Look at the history of Trump before he became President. He was responsible for paid ads wanting to condemn five young black males, the Central Park five, to death for a rape charge, only to find out later that they were exonerated, not guilty. 91 His father was a member of the Ku Klux Klan. And it continued through his Presidency. His speechwriter was a person well known for supporting a white supremacy agenda. 92 Individuals, such as David Duke, knew from his veiled remarks, that he favored white supremacy. 93 Some even committed atrocities, such as the killer in the El Paso, Texas Walmart shootings because they believed they had the President's support. 94

To the blacks, however, I would pray that they remain with a Christian attitude, such as the families of those massacred in Charleston, South Carolina on June 17, 2015 at their church. They had opened the door to their Bible study to a young 21 year old white male, who had different ideas, different attitudes. When he shot and killed seven of them and wounding one, they forgave their neighbor. Unfortunately, he hated his neighbor. 95

John Lewis continued to follow Christ's love of neighbor even though the neighbor at the Selma march for freedom yielded a baton and was trying to beat him to death.   These events are not excuses to loot or respond with any action other than a Christian response.

Justice is not the same as recompense, making up for past injustices. Justice may someday come to this country. Recompense and complete justice, I believe, will only come with Christ's kingdom.

MERCY—REPENTANT SINNERS AS A "TRIBE"

I believe that no repentant sinner should vote for Donald Trump to be our President, our chief representative. Why? Because there is a world of difference between Christ's mercy and Trump's mercy. There are two major distinctions that separate them. The first is what the mercy is. With Christ, it is divine mercy, lasting forever, endless, the eternal kingdom he promised. With Trump, the mercy is human, temporal, only for a limited number of years, during the lifetime on earth. The second major difference is in what is required to receive the pardon. With Christ, it is when we are truly sorry, sincere repentance for having acted contrary to Christ's commands of love. With Trump, repentance of having committed a crime, an act contrary to love, is not required. The only requirement is complete submission to his desires for submission to him, money and power.

Let's start with myself. To become a priest, I swore two oaths to God. One was three parts, poverty, obedience, and celibacy as a member of a religious community. The second was that I would proclaim Christ to the world as a priest and fulfill the functions of a priest. When I thought that I could no longer live up to these, I asked for a dispensation from Rome and was granted such, but the fact remains that I couldn't live up to those two oaths and I am sorry for making them.

There are other sins of which I am aware and did not receive a dispensation. At times. I forget that every gift I have is from God so I confess to pride at times, and when I was younger I also sinned against purity. But, I can say the following prayer sincerely:

> O my God, I am heartily sorry for having offended
> Thee and I detest all my sins because I dread the
> loss of heaven and the pains of hell, but most of all
> because they have offended Thee, my God, who art
> all good and deserving of all my love. I firmly
> resolve with the help of Thy grace to confess my
> sins, to do penance, and to amend my life. Amen

Christ also has one other requirement: that we forgive others for their "trespasses" against us. That I find easy to do, but some people hold on to grudges, only hurting themselves and probably not the perpetrator of the trespass. It's not worth it.

Trump unfortunately has a list of pardons for people who have never repented their crimes. He started off, correctly, I believe, by pardoning Susan B. Anthony for having voted illegally back in 1873. It's true that she never repented, but I don't believe it was a crime. Only the males of that time thought it was.

He then followed with pardons for Michael Flynn, Paul Manafort, Roger Stone, and Steve Bannon, all of whom never repented of the fraud they had perpetrated for selfish reasons and found guilty by independent juries. 96

The one person he couldn't pardon was his Vice-President, Michael Pence, from a possible death penalty for Pence's insisting on telling the truth to Congress and the American people on January 6, 2021.

Yes, there is a great difference between Christ's mercy and Trump's. I'll choose Christ's any day.

PURITY—WOMEN AS A "TRIBE"

I believe that no person who morally sees clearly should vote for Donald Trump to be our President, our chief representative. Why? Because Trump has faulty eye sight in regards to two "tribes," the first is in regards to persons of a different color than him, and secondly women. We have already considered his faulty eye sight in regards to the first, blacks and other tribes that are not white. He does not see their true worth.

His problem with women is that he has been diagnosed with an infection called "misogyny." 97 I think I heard him apologize to women for his remarks on Access Hollywood, and he sounded sincere. I hope that he was. But I have never heard an apology for the other comments demeaning women nor for defaming E. Jean Carroll. In addition, Thomas Wright in The Atlantic magazine has explained how Trump's words and actions affected Theresa May, the Prime Minister of England. He treated Angela Merkel in the same way, 98

Some Evangelical and Catholic Christians think they can choose Trump for President while recognizing his failings because he is pro-life. I do not accept that position for two reasons. First, to be truly pro life means concern about life from conception to natural death. Accepting $25,000 from the NRA to not favor laws that are against the shootings in this country indicates an

unfavorable position, more interest in money than protecting

the lives of humans already existing.. 99

As head of his party, he supports his representatives to accept the

money from the NRA instead of passing laws against "Assault"

weapons and bullet clips that account for the "mass" shootings.

How many unnecessary deaths*do we have each year because we

avoid the truth? The truth is that such laws would not interfere with

the individual American having a gun for protection or hunting

reasons.. It is obvious and undeniable.

Secondly, the anti-abortion position that Trump has seems to be

more in favor of getting votes and criminalizing women than in

supporting life.   Abortion is a moral issue between the mother

and her God. I disagree with the position that it is simply a health

issue. No, first and foremost, it is a moral matter that women have

to take seriously because it involves entire lifetimes. It can put the

mother's life and health at risk also, My wife, Paula, had ectopic

pregnancies and needed a medical doctor's assistance and care. I

also know of another woman who had a dead fetus that needed

removal. There should not be laws that are against seeking medical

advice from a doctor. It is a much more complex issue than we

admit.

Also, the laws should be to help, not to criminalize. At present, a

law in Texas gives $10,000 to a person who reports on another

 involved in an abortion.   Criminalization. Would you favor a law

giving the $10,000 to the woman who may need the money to have

the child?   100

PEACEMAKERS===POLICE AND FIRST RESPONDERS
AS A "TRIBE"

I believe that no police person or first responder should vote for
Donald Trump as our President, our chief representative? Why?
Because he seems to cause havoc, chaos wherever he goes. You,
on the contrary, probably act quickly and the more peace you bring,
the happier you are.

In reading Do Something Beautiful For God I was astounded. Here's
what Mother Teresa wrote for May 25..

> _Choose the way of peace. Let us not use bombs and
> guns to overcome the world. Let us use love and
> compassion. Peace begins with a smile. Smile five
> times a day at someone you don't really want to
> smile at. Do it for peace. Let us radiate the peace
> of God. In this way let us set the world alight with
> His light and extinguish all hatred and love of power.
> Peace in the world, yes, but first peace in our hearts.
> Do you have peace in your heart today? If not, why not?   101

My father, Y. L., was one of the first of the Illinois State Police.
He quit after a few years to form his own electrical business in our
small town. At the end of his career, the sheriff in our county was
found guilty of several crimes, so they asked Dad to serve for about
eight months. He reflected what Mother Teresa suggests. He faced
criminals with his moral strength, not with guns. He sought peace
and order.

What really astounds me in this section by Mother Teresa is the smile, five times a day, and she did. In your workday as police or medical first responders, you too have the same opportunity, and you have my respect and admiration if your response is like Mother Teresa's and Dad's.

I don't believe that Donald Trump has chosen peace or would choose it in the future. He didn't choose it on January 6, 2021, when he urged his supporters to "march' up to the Capitol or on the evening of the George Floyd protest at St. John's Church on Lafayette Square. Instead, he called for the police to "dominate" the streets in what the Anglican bishop, Marianne Budde, described as "antithetical" to Christ's teachings. 102

It's one thing to be always alert to possible evil acts against you and another to "dominate."

COURAGE---POLITICIANS AS A "TRIBE"

I believe that no politician should vote for Donald Trump as our President, our chief representative. Why? Because if they do, they're probably acting contrary to their true beliefs.

Mitch McConnell: "There is no question that President Trump is practically and morally responsible for provoking the events of that day. ... Fellow Americans beat and bloodied our own police. They stormed the Senate floor. They tried to hunt down the Speaker of the House. They built a gallows. And chanted about murdering the Vice-President." 103

William Barr......... "False claims of fraud were bullshit. My suspicion all the way along was that there was nothing there. It was all bullshit." 104

Lindsey Graham— He called Donald Trump 'a jackass' after hearing that Trump had declared John McCain not a war hero. Trump labeled Graham "an idiot." 105

2015—Graham about Trump: "He's a race-baiting, xenophobic, religious bigot. He doesn't represent my party. I don't think he has a clue about anything. He is empowering radical Islam. I would rather lose without Donald Trump than try to win with him." 106

2016 Graham about Trump: "I think he's a kook. I think he's crazy. I think he's unfit for office." 107

In 2017, Graham met with Trump at the White House and on the golf course. He reversed his position 180 degrees. "What concerns me about the American press is this endless, endless attempt to label the guy some kind of kook, not fit to be President." 108

These are just a few of the politicians who have clearly stated what they honestly think of Donald Trump.

They cannot have it both ways. Either their original statements are true or they are not. From all that Donald Trump has said and done, his words and actions, I'm inclined to believe what the politicians said before their private meeting with him on a private basis.

It requires this eighth Beatitude, Courage, to confront the fear that not acceding to Trump's agenda presents.

CONCLUSION

As America citizens, we have a very serious decision to make. Shall we choose evil or shall we choose love? Much depends upon our perspective.

If we have a limited human perspective, we will choose the evil: money, money, money, temporal power, power, power, the antithesis of the eight Beatitudes, Trump over Christ.

If we have a divine perspective, we will choose Christ and Golgotha over Trump, love over hate, unity over division. Before we look at these perspectives, there are two important points that we must have very clear in our minds.

1} Christ did not use the government to impose His commands upon us. We had to select to be with Him. "Render to Caesar the things that are Caesar's and to God the things that are God's." In our day, there are those who say we need a Christian Nationalism that imposes its will through the government on us. That is not of Christ because He gave us commands to choose to love His father, God, with all our heart, all our minds, and all our will and to love our neighbor as we love ourselves and He would determine if we were following His commands, not the government.

2} Our Constitution has a Preamble, however, that is consistent with

Christ's commands. As Americans, we are this: "We hold these truths to be self-evident, that all men are created equal, that they are endowed by their Creator with certain inherent, inalienable rights , that among these are life, liberty, and the pursuit of happiness." Please re-read this sentence and note the words: "equal", "created", "Creator", and "rights" for an unforgettable understanding because these are the Christian words that we are in danger of losing.

This is the real decision that we must make: which perspective do we have of this life? The human perspective is limited, temporal, focused on the riches of this world, money, power, control, selfishness, self-promotion, domination, autocracy.
The divine perspective is unlimited, everlasting, focused on eternal happiness, others, love, sharing, giving, unselfishness, caring, democracy.

From their words and actions, these are the choices we must make.

Jesus Christ	Donald Trump
Humility	Arrogance
Empathy	Apathy,
Meekness	Selfishness,
Justice for all	Injustice for non-whites, "White Supremacy"
Mercy for Repentance	Unmerciful, Vengeance except for his servants
Purity	Misogyny
Peacemaking	Chaos, War, Hitler, NATO to be dissolved
Courage	Fear

Many followers of Christ have failed at times to live up to Christ's commands but they didn't proclaim the opposite, the antithesis. For example, Peter, whom Christ chose to be the leader of his church, failed in courage three times the day Christ was on Golgotha---but Peter had stated clearly to Christ, "You know I love you" and at the end had the courage to be nailed upside down because of that love. Is this Christian in thought or what you want as Americans? Trump's words "When someone screws you, screw them back in spades" and "go for the jugular so that people will not mess with you." "I believe in an eye for an eye, like the Old Testament says. " 97

Trump's words: "Some of the people who forgot to lift a finger when I needed them, they need my help now, and I'm screwing them against the wall. I'm doing a number and I'm having so much fun.' 98

Yes, we are all criminals on Golgotha. We have all failed, but having eliminated the negative we can focus on our final prayer, "Lord, remember us when you enter your kingdom."

Hopefully, we have surrendered the I, me, mine and are striving for the we, us, our. This is an expression of our sentiments, our desires, our lives through the Beatitudes. Either we are wholeheartedly Christians seeking an eternal kingdom through Golgotha or we are Trumpers seeking money and temporal power through Mar-a-Lago.

NOTES

Sources for the Beatitudes: The NIV Large Print Study Bible, 10th Anniversary Edition,

The Zondervan Corporation, 1995.

1. "19 Things Donald Trump Knows Better Than Anyone Else,"

   The Washington Post, Aaron Blake, October 4, 2016

2. "Trump Declares He Is Now the Best Thing That Ever Happened

   to Puerto Rico," The New York Times, Peter Baker and Patricia

   Mazzel, September 18, 2020; "Trump Delayed $20 Billion in Aid

   to Puerto Rico," The Guardian, Coral Murphy Marcos.

3. "Did Trump Call U.S. War Dead 'Losers' and 'Suckers?, www. Vox.

   Alex Ward, September 4, 2020.

4. "Racial Views of Donald Trump." www. En. Wickipedia.Org

5. www.Cnn./"I've never done anything wrong...'

6. Judicial Pardons.org "Presidential Pardons 2016-2020."

7. www. Access Hollywood Tapes/ Bush and Trump.

8. Putin a "genius' and a "savvy" move about the invasion of the

   Ukriaine.

9. Alex Ward citation #4

10. Smithsonian Presidents, Carter Smith, Metro Books, New York, 2004, p. 190.

11. Ibid., p. 194

12. www. voicesofdemocracy.und.edu/The Four Freedoms Speech

13.. Smithsonian, pp. 192-201.

14. www. Covid 19/Trump statements.

15. www. taped interview with Bob Woodward

16. www. Covid-19/Trump statements.

17. www.bing/ "Truman, 'The Buck Stops Here'"

18. Smithsonian Presidents, p. 204.

19. Ibid., pp. 206-211.

20. www.covid 19/Trump statements.

21. www. taped interview with Bob Woodward

22. The Washington Post, "Trump made 30, 753 false or misleading claims as president. Nearly half came in his final year.." Glenn Kessler, 01-23- 2021.

23. Smithsonian Presidents, DDE, p. 216

24. Ibid, , pp. 211-216.

25. Ibid., p. 216

26.. --Ibid., pp. 214-216.

27. "19 Things Trump, knows better…"Aaron Blake.

28. "Did Trump Call U.S. War Dead 'Suckers' and 'Losers'?" www. Vox, Alex Ward, September 4, 2020.

29. Smithsonian Presidents, JFK, p.224 .

30. Ibid., p. 220.

31. Ibid. pp. 222-225.

32. The Washington Post, "The final GOP tax bill is complete. Here's what's in it." Heather Long, 12-03-17.

33. . www. ". nbcnews.com / Trump and North Korea's Kim Jung Un fell in love/ 10-02-18.

34. The Washington Post, "The final GOP tax bill…" Long

35. Smithsonian Presidents, LBJ, p.228.

36. Smithsonian Presidents, LBJ. P.226.

37. www.wikipedia.org/ racial views of Donald Trump. "

38. Ibid.

39. Smithsonian Presidents, Nixon, p. 234.

40.. Ibid., pp. 236-241.

41. www.nytimes/"The complete list of Trump's twitter insults, 2015-2021.";
www.youtube.com/ Donald Trump's   Funniest Insults."

42. Ibid.

43. Smithsonian Presidents, Ford, p. 244.

44. Ibid. . p. 242.

45.. www.wikipedia/ "United States Capitol Attacked.".

46. www. nbcnews/ "Trump says he would pardon January 6 participants"

47. www. nytimes.com,, April 16, 2017, interview with Jimmy Carter regarding
Christ.

48. Smithsonian Presidents, Carter, p. 248..

49. .Ibid., p. 246.

50. Ibid., p. 246-249.

52.   "Donald Trump: I'm not sure if I ever asked God's forgiveness,"
_____ Christian Post, Ray Nothstine, July 20, 2015.

51.   www. en.wikipedia.org/" Immigration policy of Donald Trump.";
en.wikipedia.org/Jeff Sessions.

53. Smithsonian Presidents, Reagan, p. 250.

54. www.en.wikipedia, org/ Ronald Reagan

55. Smithsonian Presidents , pp. 252-259.

56. www.en Wikipedia.org/Trump the wall

57. Ibid.

58. Smithsonian Presidents, G.H.W. Bush, p. 260.

59. Ibid, pp. 260-265

60. www.The Atlantic. Com/Trump "America First."/October 29, 2020.

61. Ibid.

62. Smithsonian Presidents, Clinton, p. 270.

63. Ibid., pp. 266-273.

64. www.npr.org/ "Why Trump's authoritarian language about vermin matters."/November 17, 2023.

65. Ibid.

66. Smithsonian Presidents, Bush, p. 278.

67. Ibid., p. 274.

68. Ibid. 274-280.

69. www.cnn.com/Trump on Jan 6 'lovefest"./July 01, 2022'; www.bbc/August 8,2021..

70. www.cbsnews.com/McConnell says Trump practically and morally responsible.

71. www. azquotes.com /Barack Obama

72. Wikipedia, Barack Obama.

73. www.cbsnews.com /"I could stand in the Middle of 5th avenue and shoot somebody...."

74. www. nbcnews/politics/ Trump scams McCain blocking Obama's Affordable Care Act

75. www. wickipedia.org/ racial views of Donald Trump/www.npr.org/ Is trump really that racist?/October 21, 2020.-

76. www. Wikipedia .org/Trump administration family separation policy..

77. www.cnn.com/ Iran analysis Trump and Raisi Iran Treaty

78. www.Trump and promise of autocratic takeover

79. www.libertystatepsrk.com/emma Grover Cleveland

80. www.Ellis island. Liberty State Park. Emma Lazarus

81. www. usatoday.com/Senator James Lankford and immigration bill/ February 8, 2024.

82. www.cnn.com/Trump "lies"/Colin Powell/Generals

83. Ibid.

84. Ibid,

85. Ibid.

86. Ibid.

87. Ibid.---

88. Mayflower, Nathaniel Philbrick, Viking Publishing, New York, 2006.

89. www. Wikipedia.org/ "The 1619 Project, Nicole Hannah-Jones,nytimes, 2019.

90. His Truth is Marching On John Lewis and the Power of Hope, Jon Meacham, Random House, New York, 2020.

91. www.Time.com/ "The Central Park Five and Donald Trump History"/ Ken Burns, Sarah Burns, David McMahon, The Central Park Five Documentary.

92. en.Wickipedia.org /Stephen Miller

93. www.vox.com/ "Why we voted for Donald Trump."/David Duke, August 12, 2017.

94. www.bbc/ el Paso Murders on August 3, 2019, a young 21 year old killed 23 persons and injured 22 others at a Walmart

95. www.wikipedia, massacre at Charleston, S.C.

96. www.justice.com/pardons granted by President Donald Trump, 2017-2021

97. "11 Ways to recognize a misogynist"/Stephanie Reeds/www.vox.com/"Donald Trump's history of misogyny, sexism, harassment" 10 8-2016, Libby Nelson.

98. www. The Atlantic/"How Trump undermined Theresa May," Thomas Wright

99. www. en.wikipedia/National rifle Association

100. www.cbsnews.com Texas law

101. Do Something Beautiful for God, Blue Sparrow, 2020., Dynamic Catholic.com

102. www.cnn.com Bishop Mariann Edgar Budde (live interview with Anderson Cooper)

103. www.cbsnews.com/ "McConnell says Trump practically and morally responsible"*/February 14, 2021

104. www.huffpost.com / Barr bullshit/ July 17, 2021.

105. www.en.wikipedia/LindseyGraham

106. Ibid

107. Ibid

108. Ibid

109. The Art of the Comeback, www. Wikipedia, Donald Trump, 1997

110. www."How Donald Trump Sees Himself," Scott Glover, 2016. ,

About the Author

He's a Christian American, born and raised in a small town in Illinois, Kankakee. After high school, he entered a Catholic religious community, the Viatorians, earned a bachelor's and master's in history at Loyola University in Chicago, was ordained a priest in 1963, served one year in Arlington Heights, Illinois and four years in Colombia, South America, as a high school teacher. In 1969, he requested and received a dispensation from Rome, returning to the laity in 1970.

In 1971, he met Paula, a former nun, and married on Watergate break-in day, June 17, 1972. In 1975, Ron and Paula adopted two children from Cambodia, a sister and brother. After a successful career in the insurance business for twenty-four years, he returned to teaching at Montgomery Community College in Rockville, Maryland, for ten years.

Ron and Paula retired to the Villages, Florida in 2007. Ron worked at the Savannah Center until 2016 when he had a cardiac arrest. Paula went to her eternal reward on Ash Wednesday, February 17, 2021.   Paula's death and Ron's cardiac arrest have helped in the perspective presented in this book.

Ron has published eight books and all should be available on Amazon.

Dear Aimee; From Faith to Love, 2017

 Let's Be Honest America: Truth and Freedom, 2020

 Truth and Consequences on Opinion Highway, 2021,

Please: Attitudes, Perspectives, Truth, Freedom, 2022

What's That? 2022

Especially for You, 2024

Others, 2024

We, Us, Our, 2024.

Printed in the United States
by Baker & Taylor Publisher Services